THE GREAT
ABORTION

THE GREAT
ABORTION

TOURVILLE DELERME JR.

ARPress
ILLUMINATING IDEAS,
EMPOWERING VOICES

ARPress
45 Dan Road Suite 5
Canton MA 02021

Hotline: 1(800) 220-7660
Fax: 1(855) 752-6001

Ordering Information:
Quantity sales. Special discounts are available on quantity purchases by corporations, associations, and others. For details, contact the publisher at the address above.

Printed in the United States of America.

| ISBN-13: | Paperback | 979-8-89389-653-4 |
| | eBook | 979-8-89389-654-1 |

Library of Congress Control Number: 2024921588

Table of Contents

A CLOSER LOOK

What a strange and curious piece of art.
The colors do not mix well and the texture is grainy.
It is a careless painting that allows for
way too much interpretation.
Sickly curators value the unsettling
disconnect it projects.
It eludes their desire for the toasty and familiar,
so they bow to it as dangerous art.
Spectators are chilled past insult.
The harmony is missing in an abrupt and obvious way.
It is thematically amputated. No
foreground, sky, or backdrop.
I can hardly make out the shadowy figures
that seem to stand by themselves.
Their body parts are not portioned out correctly.
The artist does not esteem symmetry like the greats.
This picture is a grand adventure in half effort.
I think I am close to hating this rendering.
Too many dark colors threaten to swallow
these sadly misshapen bipeds.
I will not credit them with the human
jewels of vision and hope.
They seem to be getting along with no direction or fire.
They sink into badly colored darkness as
I slowly make out an angled eyebrow fixed
on the face of one murky humaniod.

It speaks to disappointment in a way a herd of
postmodern French philosophers could only
pretend to serve up from behind a lectern.
The image begins to mouth something in a hoarse voice.
Exactly what it is, I can not say for the moment.
Yet this abominable creation of the artist
now looks upon me as a prosthetic

A HOLE

I dug a hole for no reason at all.
I grabbed my shovel as if it were a part of me.
Every scoop of dirt plugged me
deeper into a primal feeling.
With brute force I entered into the
mystery of dogs and bones;
Closer into the mouth of an unclean motivation.
Each time I stabbed the earth with
my shovel I caught a shiver.
Helpless worms met a vengeful god that day.
I felt an intoxicating violence that was the truth of life.
So vicious was my desire that was not for oil or treasure.
I kept digging until I struck a light orange hardness.
The loose soil gave way to something more serious.
No more black cake to rip through with joy.
This was the material upon death
marches of invading armies.
It held up churches and whorhoses with no distinction.
Neither deluge or explosive has triumphed over it.
My shovel began to bend.
This layer seemed to stare back at me.
My soul became disturbed at this defiant sediment.
The next day I bought a drill and put it to work.
The criminal feeling returned, that of a cruel master.
The excavation of a hidden world not my
own made me glad and strong.

Then an evil thing happened.
The battery of my drill dipped in energy
and the speed of it began to wane.
A drill that once spun furiously with a
mechanistic guarantee bowed before soil
that swallowed our grandparents.
At this realization I did a cowardly thing.
I took the exhumed patches of dirt
and began to fill up the hole.

A NEW IDEA

I will trot my fox out before the council knowing full
well there is a team of hounds poised to crush her.
When the bugle blows, and the committee
roars at the rush of the chase, I will
command my fox to stay and not run.
She will lick her paws with royal disinterest as her
assassins trample rose and weed to utterly destroy her.
Vicious dogs out to bite and tear is nothing novel,
but a fox that houses no retreat in her body is the
eye of God and the first draft of a revolution.

A MATTER OF FORCE

I stand over mankind with a hammer.
The sun makes him soft, and in the
shade he practices renunciation.
I sneak fire into his nostrils during slumber that
he may feel as a conqueror when he sneezes.
To induce fragility, I must inch him
near the sweetness of life.
Deep aspiration forms parallel to his point of fracture.
Every time he is made to hope in
progress I bring the mallet up.
It can take up to a calendar year to
achieve perfect extension.
I stood by him through every pay raise,
baby shower, and evil report.
When he splatters, I can tell you what
pieces will fly in what direction.
How many nights does it take for
a melon to become ripe?
I allot him a season of grief to peel back
his blessings like an ear of corn.
I will shake him with trial then put my ear to his lungs.
Find what a man loves most, then stretch him like clay.
He will try to maintain the original order out
of which sprung mirth and talebaring.

Remove his honeycomb and he will dry up with spite.
Once he swears the oath he cannot perform, hold
your peace and you will hear my practice swing.

BULLFROG

History has turned another card in our game.
Braver creatures slumber for a time while
circumstance ordained slippery new overlords.
It is the era of the Bullfrogs.
A time when men beguile with a puffed out chest.
They croak out edicts to jaws suited
to devour them in two bites.
Understanding their reign as terrific and
ephemeral accidents, they line up their
lily pads for an inevitable retreat.
Bullfrog's must cloak their hind legs.
Nature witnesses against the uncertain
with a prominent back foot.
From swamp lands to forests, be it jungles or
plains, all domains know that the vulnerable favor
the hind leg when their rank is challenged.
Never trust a creature that negotiates the two worlds
of water and land. They try to master one and play
house guest to the other being welcomed in neither.
How did such a meek life gain stewardship?
They snuck a ride on the backs of grander
beasts. Cleaning mites out of their regal coats
was the birthplace of their command.
To ruin the sleep of our amphibian overlords,
one must dare him to justify his standing.

Oust them after their service is complete,
or they will sanction your coming and
going, and put you under tribute.

BACHA'S FREEDOM

Bacha, do you know that you are free?
We will no longer watch or advise you.
Your diet is now a private matter.
You may eat your brownie or throw it away.
I will not comb your hair, nor will
I assist you in washing up.
Mary will explain things to you
only if you ask her to do so.
Be warned Bacha, we can now say no to you.
Put away your memory of our perpetual softness.
Freedom is cold and wearisome. You
must remember or perish.
Work hard that you may not be
condemned to uncaring corners.
Trust selectively with your money, or
come to know debt as a brother.
Freedom is portioned out liberally to the aimless rabble.
Order and restriction is reserved for the crown.
How far do you intend to push this novelty?
Will you choose your own tie?
Watch television whenever you feel like it?
Mary will not sing to you as she once did.
Do you think all of our actions were driven by love?
The rent is high good friend and we do as we are told.
Welcome to a serrated freedom that can
pronounce your name forward and backward.

Do not slip up in thinking a smile will mend
any damage, because freedom will call you
out and expect immediate payment.

CHILDREN OF THE NEW WINE

We are the fresh sting of mint.
Our long stem roses shall scent the
necks of your wives just fine.
We fly over your lakefront property
to worship in the mountains.
Our breasts are red and our eyes glimmer black.
You can graze our backs but never
achieve the steady shot.
The cooking pot shall remain empty.
The scarecrow does not turn us away as we perch
upon the headstones of your grandfathers.
Underneath your family crest do we fall over naked and
dizzy. It is our joke to pledge loyalty under intoxication.
We don't fear your high positions.
Pay us in fruit, see if we care.
We shall break your silly currency anyway.
We bath twice as much as your kind, eat three
times more, and look four times better.
Apply for membership to our guild and we
will laugh your tribe out of existence.

FAMILIAR STRANGERS

Only on earth do we cross swords
racing our wives to a black veil.
Ghoulish acts of violence are carried out
for the preservation of surnames.
It is a subterranean religion that
gnaws upon the conscience.
If I have not made a crib for my baby out of
the bones of suspicious tribes, am I a man?
What is the sickness that owns our hands?
Crush and dominate speak this unseen master.
In heaven we drank from the same
river of light as brothers.
Now I raise my flag in defiance of yours.
And you block the marriage of our children.
If only I could pass back through the fog of
forgetfulness and reclaim my brother.
It was only yesterday that we were
bounding and wrestling like bear cubs
before the Holy One in complete joy.
We are divine shapeshifters that have
decided upon enemy forms.
Now it is the bridge of your nose that I hate and
it is the curl of my hair that you distrust.
But I exhort you to remember when we
raced angels and lost with laughter.

We sat at the dazzling theater of creation
without bathroom breaks.
Recall how you dared the void to be what it was not,
and it obliged with an explosion of gas, fire, and ice.
How we fled our underestimation that day.
Yet we have agreed to meet like this; I
at your neck and you at my heel.

FIRED FROM MY LIFE.

Take my son to the park.
Care to touch my wife in bed; she needs reassurance.
Sign my checks legibly as I never did.
It was all a confusing dream and you may step into it.
It is no longer my responsibility.
Adjust the temperature; it's your house now.
Go to church like I would have given the foresight.
If you see the pastor, tell him I was
not right for the part.
Take me over; seize my possessions.
Taylor my clothes to your shape.
My sisters will never love or even like you.
They will not go along with the
conditions of my termination.
Don't isolate yourself; that is what did me in.
Suffer your neighbors when they need an ear.
You can cry now and again, just not before women.
Don't entertain a thousand crushes.
Let only one woman enchant you, that
is how you will meet my wife.
You will have to do it all over again.
Everything I missed I want you to
try to get with both hands.
Even if you fail, chase dreams until your legs give out.
Have more sex; God will not begrudge you.

Cut class with a plan in mind. What you do must
not fall beneath the worthiness of a scrapbook
Don't blow all your money to run from problems,
it is much cheaper to just run from them.
Okay then, I suppose that's enough.
Here are the keys to my life, be reckless.

HUMAN BATTERIES

Carry, type, and speak you speakers.
Move and halt upon our command.
What dumb and wonderfully useful power.
Like gunpowder before the shell casing.
Let us direct that power before they
grey and bend beyond use.
Wash the hands of our shareholders twice before
looking upon their broken bodies once.
Douse them in caffeine that they might
fulfill their quotas of shiny and new.
Bath unit two in fluorescent lighting
and they will stop complaining.
Uniforms make them feel a part of
something bigger. Choose a solid color.
We don't want to mock their professional
sensibilities with preschool pastels.
If they become lax in their duties, we will
install cameras in their dental fillings.
We make no distinction between
junkies, derelicts, and part-timers.
We only promote gods of labor.
Let Buddah sit, Christ die, and Moses play
with water; you shall only pay homage to
deities that toil through highdays
All recycle bins double for the suggestion box.

You near the end of your robust ten minute break, run to your works station or it will come out of your vacation.

MAN EATER

My wife has been eaten and nothing remains to
celebrate her memory. Beset by learning centers,
she stood as a delectable spread of blood and fat.
I cry when I see my only daughter being
seasoned by workers bearing official seals.
They carry a variety of degrees, but
in the end they are all chiefs.
My father looks in vain for his missing arm.
Strong and zesty, he is not a man of meek flavor.
Only a select few had courage enough to
tear his limb off. It will be said of him that
he had an exceptional serving size.
He will simply be picked apart by
choosier tastes with stronger jaws.
Whole towns are populated by faces disfigured
from digestive juices of these monsters.
The acidic dissolution is slow giving us
time to say goodbye to one another.
These ferocious buildings bite and gnaw.
Dangerous beliefs swallow.
Authorities marched us into a cauldron
and called it stability.
We walked along adult lions and never was the wiser.

LEOPARD KING

Imagine an arboreal master capable of
painting rows of branches blood red.
A ghost beneath the wheat materializing
at will to take his pick of grazers.
A solo act of curiosity can shut down safari
with mothers scrambling to locate their
children. Black speckled against the gold is not
camouflage but a five minute head start.
A killer's killer works out of a conspicuous dog dare.
He courts eyewitness, and should a gust of wind
knock down his wanted poster, he would hang it
back up again. Only making room for the slack
jaw lion, a leopard is perfect in his domain.
For all this the Almighty has shown me that
he will fall by the cunning of a fleet footed
rabbit. How can a power so thorough be
outdone by a delicate hop and nibble?
He will fall to it and may not rise up again.
For this cause I will inspect every dropping of
dung, fall upon every elongated ear, and uproot
all shrubbery. Try as I may, my demise comes
not by a bushy mane, but by a fluffy tail.
The indignity of it all.

THE HOLY PLACE

You thought nothing of polluting my temple
with the custom of unwashed masses.
In your heart was no ambition for gold, neither
did your eyes enlarge upon the sight of spears
of ivory. Your trespass was merely an answer
to hard rain driven by an east wind.
I could have put you out for the filth
you trafficked into my holy place.
The law of heaven would have justified me
in laying thirty nine stripes to your back save
one. Watching you use the cloth from the
altar to dry yourself moved me to mercy.
It did quell your shiver.
Upon lifting your head you saw all
manner of precious substance.
Yet the portion you sought was warmth and
a temporary reprieve from the elements.
For this cause I escorted you into rooms
never seen before by heathen pilgrims.
I taught you a new alphabet and unrolled
manuscripts zealously guarded by the ancients.
The expense of having you clad in the
best garments was little to me.
And just when I thought the light of your eye
reflected the brilliance of an adept worthy of high
degree did you blaspheme with foreign worship.

With a sharp stone you cut yourself
bleeding in supplication to Astaroth.
You howled like a coyote and petitioned for bone soup.
It was too much of an ask that you rise
above your provincial stain.
The remains of your beggarly culture is moth
eaten and open to the blast of mildew.
Let the mud cleave to your sandals once more.
Be rinsed anew in unrelenting downpour.
Have your fill of bitter cold and dark clouds.
Orphan thou art and orphan shalt thou remain.

HOOK OVER HEART

I place no faith in romantic love.
It is enough for me to put my hooks in whomever I will.
With one thought I can activate crescent
prongs embedded over ten years ago.
Can you feel a tug upon your flesh?
A faint itch gives way to a gentile pulling.
Imagine a hook that lies so dormant that
your blood has forgotten how to fight it.
Let the true paramour fumble stupidly over roses.
I draw, and the pierced one comes. It is that simple.

CITADEL FLOOR

I will purify my Citadel.
The mocking tongue shall be cast out.
Let all traitors be burned with fire.
I will no longer pollute myself with
the conniving scoundrel.
I will put down all sneers with a hot iron.
The false ones shall be as a morbid decoration
at the base of my encampment. I will
festoon the trees with backbiter bones.
My fortress will be strong from within.
Let the terror remain from without.
I thank my Heavenly Father for the
will to purge my citadel.
Observe the thrown palm branches to reinforce it's
rampart with the blessing of the Nazarene. It is honor
to the Paraclete when I sever the canker worm in two.
A moment of harshness enacted from the
inside ensures months of tranquility.
Outside my walls is the cruelty of a forever winter.

100 LEAGUES

First they denied the existence of waters so dark
that the fabled Narcissist should weep.
The mere mention of such an opaque body
caused them to trade incredulous looks.
Perhaps they thought it was a bit of theater that
I slid all their pictures of Aruba back across
the table. Pray to a holy God that the waters I
speak of are not moved out of their place.
Chide as they did, I informed them of waves
with no give; waves that could not be read.
Any guide promising safe passage through it dare not
sail with the adventurers of his encouragement. Oh
uncharitable water, you give up neither crab or fish.
What living can be made upon this sea?
Even the channel leading to it hisses as a coiled viper.
Those looking for summer fun are
turned back with one glance.
It wasn›t enough for me to tell them
of it's sudden caprice.
I warned them of it's indifference, yet they
needed to trouble it with canoe and ore.
The lovers of frontier can only tilt right
on their vow for better or worse.

What is thy testimony from 100 leagues beneath?
The ripple of onyx is a deceiver to all search parties.
It is as if they never were.

MY EYE IS PERFECT

Those desiring to touch me must count
the cost of a thousand step ladders.
My ear is a privilege of happenstance
and furious knowledge.
Only through mercy has it become
a thing of public domain.
My eye is not subject to fair use, but I made
it common to transform the commoner.
Yet will I now sequester the hearts of my choosing
from behind an impenetrable wall of elitism.
My care is a goodly diamond fetching sums
that could rub up against state budgets.
It has received enough scratches to authenticate
it, but shall not receive one more over to decimate
it's value. The sun is not nourished by flowers.
Let every stem and petal learn this
lesson after the rainfall.
Can the vine instruct a ball of fire how to conduct itself?
Should such a star play student to the lecture of trees?
My division is cruel and uneven.
I will temper my heat that few may blossom,
but to the many do I show myself as a glowing
furnace of never ending appetite.

BE MY GUEST

You can not transgress a boundary to then
demand that yours be honored.
It is the folly of burglars objecting to wall paper.
You are here under an auspicious star
of mercy and not by invitation.
Through stealth you had hoped to spoil my house.
This illegal collection of my goods was permitted that I
may seize upon your traumas, insecurities, and deficits.
They are my watercolors.
I purchased them with every conversation you
eavesdrop on between me and my family, with every
thought you gasp at, with every prayer you stole.
What you meant for robbery I turned
into a fair and equal exchange.
Your nerve endings are now my intellectual property.
Was it I that sought after you, or was the
map and compass on your person?
Climb inside the leopard's enclosure if you will,
just do not sob over personal space and an article
of rights. You paid tickets for the public exhibition,
but you wanted more, a private showing.
I do whatever I please.
The cry of avenging women is a decibel
beneath my auditory range.
Oh Gorgon sisters, let down your snakes.
Bonnets are not supposed to wriggle with motion.

My minstrel is not allowed to leave.
She can speak in chords.
If I wish to add the young one to my museum,
you will do absolutely nothing but watch
through your heart shaped glasses.
Never pretend to know what I am or
feign understanding as to what I want
unless it comes from my lips.

FORGOTTEN

I can hide a kiss of peace at the end of my
ire, or make the entire experience of my
visitation melt away like a fever dream.
Have you looked upon my separated company who
are driven to their knees with a stabbing deja vu?
They muster up the powers of their imagination
to piece together the thing I have washed clean.
I am a launderer par excellence.
Go to, search out blot or wrinkle, your mind
is given back to you folded and clean.
The remembrance of me has vanished.
Try as you may, the piercing scent of my
fuller's soap interrupts reminiscing.
You tremble at the vision of black rosettes
upon gold and can't understand why.
You judged me dirty and so I have cleaned your
memory with an unforgiving stringent.
In me you saw stains so unsightly that you
put it to my awareness at every chance.
You sought to lift yourself high. How you
delighted in making a line between you and me,
and so I have washed you of any trace of me.
Tell me, do the pangs of sullenness call
out to you in the midnight hour?
It gave your wares a peculiar character,
a distinguishing charm.

Well you are made clean now, and the clean
need not judge before cleanliness.
Where do wandering feelings of the upright go
after being orphaned by the condemned.
Past the last kiss is a final detergent to make
the robes of judges painfully clean.

A GREAT AND NOTABLE DAY

You can not make a deal with the storm.
I have known men to entertain delusions of control so
hardily that they would waive their insurance policy.
They count themselves as a blood relative to the terror.
This unwelcome break in nature cares
nothing for their social standing.
What is even funnier is that they attempt
to cajole it with their approval.
A destruction that erases state surplus and bursts
the damn is now to fetch your slippers?
I tell you that the tempest shall pass over their
adorable rule book of improprieties.
It is not backed down by charges of hypocrisy,
nor can it be enticed with praise of strength.
Property rights along with scheduled holidays and
precious lives are all game pieces before it's might.
Yet men persist in trying to leash a typhoon. Show
me one hailstorm that enlists a defense attorney?
Do you know of one avalanche to rumble
inside the parameters of a publicist?
When the thunder crashes and the lightning
falls, all contracts are annulled.
"I have no partnership with men," declares the storm.
"Do not recite your code of ethics to me.
My arrival and departure has nothing
to do with your terms.

I will get me honor upon backbiters, mockers,
and all manner of decadent folk.
I will get me honor upon every house of
rebellion, every hideout of the clever, and
every stronghold of ruling classes.
Chase the storm or survive it, but you can never direct it!

ETHIOPIAN

To the adept and adversary alike, my blood
is pulled from two divergent lands.
It rushes fiercely Haitian with a
pleasant French undercurrent.
Though it coagulates in Hispaniola, and thins
out around Paris, I am frighteningly Ethiopian in
spirit. When I enter the marketplace, let the men
of high degree shout, "There goest the Ethiopian!"
When I walk before the dregs of society in the
alley ways, let them cry out, "What has thou
to do with us O Ethiopian, is our tax due?
We shall forgo bread and digest a stone
until your balance sheet is reconciled."
To the woman sprawled out before me in perfect
submission, let her ask, "What is thy desire Ethiopian?"
In warfare, let the infantry take one step as if they
took ten. Let the enemy utter to his comrades,
«Settle your affairs with your God; tonight we
battle the Ethiopians and die honorable men.

Before the Egyptian put on his skirt, all those who
stood before the Ethiopian became a cup of trembling.

COLD SPOT

I fear there is an aperture in my spirit
that can not be located.
Any house that suffers a breach loses
the fight over room temperature.
I can not hold on to surging states of euphoria, nor can
I insulate against the outside tapping melancholy.
Though I sleep with a putty knife, and wake
beside plywood, the work of a slow leak goes on
unabated. Just like that, chill replaces warmth,
and fragrance is traded in for stench.
My beauty index vanishes.
I can not distinguish the root of a rose from it's pedals.
Questions no longer connect me to knowledge
but only fertilize all of my terrors.
I become small and hateful.
Even the pilot light of my imagination is blown out.
I grope for pleasure only to finger the
edges of hibernating dives.
My meat tastes like the bark of a tree in my mouth.
Suddenly, through some act of clemency,
the billowing smoke of certainty and
meaning fills my house once more.
I can sire a griffin, or tame a pride of lions.
Benevolence is mine, and trust when I tell
you that my violence is not rented.
I can feed an orphanage or burn a village to the floor.

The power that courses through me does so
as if I never knew anything differently.
For this reason I implore the innocent
to stay away from me.
I will only put them to flight when the
direction of breeze changes.

BORN OUT OF DUE TIME

The plague has taught me one thing
plainly; we are aristocrats by nature.
We know well how to redeem endless
stretches of leisure without ruin.
How is it you have been put to
contract and I to a time clock.
It is not only wage labor that is repugnant
to me, I also hiss at the contract.
We ought to have our hands freed to
be the torches of humanity.
It is our rightful service.
Our truest productivity is not in sweat and
grunts, but in illumination and beauty.
We make it so that that the oarsmen
can row without feeling it.
The mason builds because we take
away his sense of time.
Howbeit, I leave you to furrow my
brow and scrape my knuckles.

MY PIG

What should be said of this boorish wonder?
She wishes noting more than to be seen,
even when she hides from me.
Maybe I will toss her an apple and rub her tummy.
My pig has her suitors and yet she clings to my
leg as if I should mingle with a beast muddy and
wild. Why are holy books so suspicious of you?
I know you want to think your voice is clear
and sensible as mine, but the world only
knows you for shrill grunts and squeals.
It is competition against the bleating of sheep.
I gather those horrid echoes and
attribute meaning to them.
From the moment your eyes befell me,
you moved me with a need.
In me you did see a lake the buoyancy of which
removed your self awareness in exchange for lightness.
And she became that which none could gainsay.
In me she knew a peace most pigs
could not come to know.
I spoke to her after the manner of dreams.
She acted as a pup licking my palm and rushing
to see me with the cool touch of domestication.
So I feed, spoke, and on days of madness
developed feelings of friendship for her.

Then as nature can never be thwarted, she
    bit my friend, and I made light of it.
Then she bit me, with an instant regret.
The door to her pen remains wide open,
    and my intention all too clear.
I shall miss my stout garish companion.

PEPPERMINTPOLICE

We make it unbearable for you to frown.
Is it too much of an imposition to travel with
you so that you may not feel alone?
We wrest the humor from your accounts of grief.
Asking you about your wellbeing, we arm
ourselves against the wrong reply.
You are well! You just don't know it, and life
is swelling with our officers to show you.
Is it right that you look away to
avoid returning our smiles?
You can not run from all public events stilly.
We march with good will and extra
change for you to borrow.
No, you go first, even if it inconveniences you.
Listen to one last joke and jumpstart a laugh.
We must pat you on your back so
you can feel our approval.
It is not enough that our smiles burn
into the back of your neck.
Remember, nobody is perfect for all
future mistakes you make.
We forgive your poor manners as long as you
can suffer our reminding you every minute.

Isn't this a great country? You get to
feel good even by majority vote.
Our positive malita wants to enlist you.
Don't slouch, you make us think you are sad.

SHOPKEEPER

Prepare my silver pieces in neat stacks.
I shall treat you to the greatest play.
The stage is our friendship, and the curtain is your back.
Remember all promises I made to you in
the sun are not binding in the shade.
I have always hated you.
You appear smarter, possessing a unique look.
Marked with a special style of speech,
they clamor to the point of injury.
Each time we stood together, I lost inches
in character and yards in presence.
Behold, I make us even with false agreement.
If you love classical music, I have two concert tickets.
If you oppose the war, I will hold your picket sign.
I will remain Catholic until you
lose favor with the pope.
I will be a peddler of weeds, if flowers
overpower your cologne.
The ones you love, truly I love as well.
The only difference is that I can watch
you suffer and not lose my count.
I can hear you wail and still have all
my decimals in the right place.

I will survive by my silver pieces until
they make me your benefactor.
Behold, I make us even until the glare
from my coins make you no more.

NO CIGARS

Good girls, all of them really.
They eat, think, and play together wonderfully.
A few of them know karate, others
practice their long division.
Fat, angry, tall, athletic, giddy, and curious.
One can only graze the rainbow of their depth.
They munch away at their borders, and giggle
as the crumbs fall on their blouses.
If you slight one, all incur the offense.
They groom constantly with devices most odd.
They look so good that we hold back our violence.
It is a wise decision on our part.
For they know only a revenge that is put
together one toothpick at a time until you
wake up with your neck in the stocks.
We are made bigger by their company.
Any experience is not worth having
if we cannot tell them.
Why did we ever ruin them with laws?

OATH

With my right hand over my heart, I
swear not to see a damn thing.
I do not witness children pass out from
hunger and untreated disease.
Nor the bloody ku that we orchestrated
for the captains of industry.
My ears wax dull at the stories of herdsmen not
allowed to drink from their own rivers.
I can not see the unending fire coming out
of gun nozzles when my package arrives.
I vow blindness to the collapse of their markets
and the flickering promise of a debt forgiveness.
Supposedly a report came out yesterday about human
rights abuses of dark workers on a soil not my own.
I can honestly say I was watching a
grasshopper when it aired.
I never saw nations made to tailor law and
custom to receive our medicine.
Genocide, what genocide?
All of it is rubbish to Saint Thomas and I.

SMALL MEN

There is something eternally out of place with
the small man from his scrappy demeanor
to his large ambition for conquest.
He dreams outside of what his little body deserves.
They are truly unsettling tugging at our
waists to warm our hearts with jokes.
Perhaps to gain a few inches by a solicitor's charm.
Yet they make us sad as they don children's
wear trying desperately to move like men.
Respect slides into hiding when a woman must bend
the knee to kiss a stout companion giving her the look
of mother before she is ready to assume that identity.
It is through their mouths that they
project broad shoulders.
Just as they almost have us deceived, they
are seated with an obstructed view. They are
pressed into a light jog when walking beside
us breaking any spell they cast on us.
Can such a population ever touch command,
perhaps influence, but command is far
removed from noisy stubby things.
Skilled taylors can do nothing to mask
the theft of their endowment.
Consign them to the woods and pray for wolves.

STRANGE MONKEY

The Nile hates you, drink carefully.
Body snatching crocks are watching
you without clemency.
The swarms are ever present, these thieves
already have a quarter of your blood.
Even though you meander crookedly, step
lightly, for thorn baring flowers position
themselves that you might howl at a mistep.
The golden beast will take you at
the bottom of that minute.
If the pride advances upon you, the
hyenas will count your bones.
The gibbons keep watch testifying against
you in the trees with screeching.
Your eyes are different from the
rest, small and intelligent.
The Nile has never seen two feet
outside the guild of birds.
You seem greedy and unpredictable.
The Nile is not familiar with your program.
How you mate, fight, and establish
territory is all very erratic.
She does notice the dedication you
have toward your tools.
Ever since that queer hobby has become your focus,
the number of buffalo has dropped dramatically.

The Nile has seen the monkey; you are not the monkey.
Yet it sees flashes of the same deviations in you both.
Fire comes from the skies, and now
you bring it out of sticks.
Guard yourself strange monkey, more species
have vanished for half the infraction of magic.
The penalty for making the Nile uneasy is extinction.
Her sharp distaste for you is only matched,
if not surpassed by an increasing curiosity
around your clumsiness touching instict.
Your place here can be contested
with flooding or drought.
So honor the Nile and be on your way!